Rukhsana Ahmad

Rukhsana has written and adapted many plays for stage and BBC Radio. *River on Fire* was a finalist in the Susan Smith Blackburn Awards, *Wide Sargasso Sea* was a finalist for the Writers' Guild Award for Best Radio Adaptation and *Song for a Sanctuary* was a finalist for the CRE award for best original radio drama and is published in the anthology *Six Plays by Black and Asian Women Writers* (Aurora Metro). Other plays include *Mistaken: Annie Besant in India* (Aurora Metro) and *Letting Go*.

She has also written fiction: *The Hope Chest* and *The Gatekeeper's Wife and other stories*. Rukhsana edited and translated *We Sinful Women*, a collection of contemporary Urdu feminist poetry and *The One Who Did Not Ask* by Altaf Fatima. www.rukhsanaahmad.com

First published in the UK in 2019 by Aurora Metro Publications Ltd.

67 Grove Avenue, Twickenham, TW1 4HX

www.aurorametro.com   info@aurorametro.com

T @aurorametro FB/AuroraMetroBooks

Homing Birds copyright © 2019 Rukhsana Ahmad

Cover image copyright © 2019 Luke Wakeman

With many thanks to: Marina Tuffier and Naveed Ashraf.

Printed in the UK by 4edge Limited.

ISBNs:

978-1-912430-45-1(print)

978-1- 912430-46-8 (ebook)

Homing Birds

by

Rukhsana Ahmad

for all refugees

AURORA METRO BOOKS

Intrepid plays by fearless women since 1991

Kali Theatre develops and tours ground-breaking, thought-provoking, contemporary theatre by women writers of South Asian descent.

The company seeks out and nurtures talented writers, bringing their experience and stories to audiences from all backgrounds to transform the theatre landscape and better reflect modern Britain.

Kali has been championing women writers from a South Asian background for over twenty-five years. The company actively encourages both writers and audience to reinvent and reshape the theatrical agenda, and they have gained a reputation for putting challenging issues on stage to create engaging and inspiring new theatre.

Kali's new Discovery and Festival Writer Development Programmes encourage and support the creation of new work through writing workshops, dramaturgical input and public readings, while their tours take this work to audiences across the UK.

Find our more and join the mailing list at
kalitheatre.co.uk

Email us info@kalitheatre.co.uk

Like us on facebook.com/kalitheatureUK

Follow us @KaliTheatreUK

Homing Birds

Raabia	Suzanne Ahmet
Nazneen	Mona Khalili
Michael	John O'Mahony
Saeed	Jay Varsani
Director	Helena Bell
Writer	Rukhsana Ahmad
Designer	Helen Coyston
Lighting Designer	Tanya Stephenson
Sound Designer	Dinah Mullen
Associate Director	Sita Thomas
Production Manager	Alex Ralls
Tour Stage Manager	Jessica Thanki
London Stage Manager	Amy-Marie Field
Assistant Stage Manager	Chris Grogan
Dramaturg	Suzanne Bell
Dialect Coach	Dewi Hughes
Afghanistan Consultant	Nushin Arbabzadah
Artistic Director	Helena Bell
Executive Director	Christopher Corner
Administrator	Naomi Joseph
Publicist	Nancy Poole
Marketing Manager	Rasheed Rahman
Audience Development	Hardish Virk
Casting Support	Komal Amin

Suzanne Ahmet – Raabia

Theatre includes: *Peter Pan* and *Saint George and The Dragon* (The National Theatre), *Hard Times* and *They Don't Pay? We Won't Pay!* (Northern Broadsides), *The Winter's Tale* (Sheffield Crucible), *Much Ado About Nothing* and *Dangerous Corner* (Theatre Royal, Bury St Edmunds), *I Capture The Castle* (Watford Palace/Bolton Octagon), *The Hoard Festival, Around The World In 80 Days, Arabian Nights* (New Vic, Stoke) and *The Light Princess* (The Tobacco Factory/Peepolykus). TV includes: *Adult Material, Gittins* (C4), *Doctors* and *Jonathan Creek* (BBC). She has taken part in rehearsed readings for Shakespeare's Globe and development workshops for the RSC.

Mona Khalili – Nazneen

Mona is an actor, director and writer from London. She trained with the National Youth Theatre, where she played one of the leads in *Our Days of Rage* and the title role in *Chloe Can*. Theatre includes: *Silk Moth* (Arcola), *Silently Hoping* (Vault Festival), *Spengul's Mum: Sahar Speaks* (Theatre503), *She is Taken Lightly* (Katzspace Theatre), *Titus Andronicus* (Vanbrugh Theatre), *Dancing to the Blast* (Camden People's Theatre), *Wasted* (Studio Soho), *Aya* (Bread & Roses Theatre). TV includes: *How they caught: Story of Shafilea* (BBC). Film includes: *Desert Dancer, Mona's Reading* and *Telstar*.

John O'Mahony – Michael

John's 40 year performing career includes theatre, TV, film, radio, audiobooks, training programmes and music videos. Recently he played the Seanchai (Storyteller) Fergal Monaghan in Lizzie Nunnery's *Intemperance* (New Vic Theatre). Prior to that he was Marley and a host of characters in Dickens' *A Christmas Carol* (Glasgow Citizens), Ian and the Chorus in Zinnie Harris' *This Restless*

House (The Oresteia at the Edinburgh International Festival). TV includes: *Father Ted, Mrs Brown's Boys* and *The Good Karma Hospital.* Film includes: John Bradshaw in *Babel*, Sully in *Miracle Landing on the Hudson* and the eponymous lead in the mockumentary *A Short Film About John Bolton.*

Jay Varsani – Saeed

Jay trained at East 15 Drama School. Theatre while training includes: *The Pillow Man*, (John Kazek); *Hamlet*, (Jeremy Mortimer); *Wild Honey*, (John Gillett); *All My Sons*, (Charlotte Thompson); *Jerusalem*, (Gerry Mcalpine); *The Invisible*, (Charlotte Thompson); *Blue Stockings*,(Charlotte Thompson); *The Theatre Of Illusion*, (Jules Tipton); *Freuds* (Andrew Norton). Other theatre includes: *My Beautiful Laundrette* (Leicester Curve); *Raleigh: The Treason Trial* (Shakespeare's Globe); *Memoirs Of An Asian Football Casual* (Leicester Curve); *Eastwood Ho* (Shakespeare's Globe). TV includes: *World On Fire* (Mammoth Screen); *Ripper Street* (Tiger Aspect Productions). Film credits include: *Gloves Off* (Molifilms Entertainment); *Golden Years* (Molifilms Entertainment).

Helena Bell – Director

Artistic Director of Kali since 2016. Productions include *Sundowning* by Nessah Muthy; *Ready or Not* by Naylah Ahmed and Rukhsana Ahmad's acclaimed *River on Fire*, shortlisted for the Susan Smith Blackburn Award (Lyric Hammersmith & UK tour). Prior to Kali, Helena was AD of Pursued by a Bear Productions, a new writing company resident at Farnham Maltings. Productions include *The Lamellar Project* by Grant Watson, an international, multi award-winning play for Skype (Arcola Theatre & US transfer); *Kabaddi Kabaddi Kabaddi* by Satinder Chohan (Arcola/UK tour) and *Kalashnikov – in the Woods* by the Lake by Fraser Grace (Mercury,Colchester/Theatre 503). Prior to this, Helena was Co-Artistic Director of Brighton's Alarmist Theatre. Notable productions: *Fossil Woman* by Louise Warren (Lyric Hammersmith) and *The Bedbug*, British Council tour to Russia. Helena has been a regular Guest Director at Drama Studio, London, ALRA and Mountview Drama Schools. In 1996, she was the recipient of a prestigious Arts Council Director's Bursary, specialising in New Writing

Sita Thomas – Associate Director

Sita has directed short plays at the National Theatre, Rich Mix, Southwark Playhouse, RADA and Old Vic. She is developing *Queer Tales* with the support of MGCfutures and Arts Council Wales. Theatre as Director: *The Rose and the Bulbul* (Stockwood Park, Horniman and Geffrye Museums). As Staff Director: *Top Girls* (National Theatre). As Associate Director: *Bitched* (Tristan Bates); *Zigger Zagger* (Wilton's Musical Hall). As Assistant Director: *Pity* (Royal Court); *Mass* (Southbank Centre); *Peter Pan Goes Wrong* (UK Tour). Sita holds a PhD from the University of Warwick and a Masters in Movement Direction from Royal Central School of Speech and Drama.

Helen Coyston – Designer

Recent credits include: *Operation Mincemeat* (New Diorama Theatre); *Everything I see Swallow* (The Lowry/ Summerhall); *Stepping Out* (Stephen Joseph Theatre); *The Art of Gaman* (Theatre 503); *The Wizard of Oz* (Taunton Brewhouse); *Feed* (The Lowry/Pleasance) *Sex with Robots and Other Devices* (King's Head Theatre); *A (Scarborough) Christmas Carol, The 39 Steps, Build A Rocket, Goth Weekend* (Stephen Joseph Theatre); *Our Mutual Friend* (Hull Truck); *Antigone* (UK tour); *The Acedian Pirates* (Theatre 503); *My Mother Said I Never*

Should (St James Theatre); *Made up Stories From my Unmade Bed* (Lyric Hammersmith/Latitude Festival); *Peter Pan, Watership Down, There is a War* (Watford Palace Theatre); *Bluebird* (Edinburgh Fringe).

Tanya Stephenson – Lighting Designer

A Lighting Designer with an MA in Advanced Theatre Practice from Central School of Speech and Drama and a BA in Performance Design from University of Leeds. She won the Francis Reid Lighting Design Award in 2010 and has since worked nationally and internationally with companies such as Fuel, Theatre Rites, Gecko, BBC, Paines Plough, Punchdrunk, Nevill Holt Opera, Engineer, Little Bulb, Wardrobe Ensemble, Pecho Mama, Spymonkey, Little Angel Theatre, Polka Theatre and Stomp. Outside of TV and Theatre, she has designed installations at British Library, music festivals, and has led artistic workshops with ex-offenders and prisoners.

Dinah Mullen – Sound Designer

Dinah creates sound and music for performance, specialising in collaborative projects. Theatre includes: *Keith?, The Daughter In Law, Insignificance, Richard III, The Plague, The Blue Hour of Natalie Barney* (Arcola); *Roller* (Barbican Pit); *Stella* (Brighton Theatre Royal, Hoxton Hall, Brakke Grond, Holland Festival); *Asphalt Kiss, Theseus Beefcake* (New Diorama); *Sundowning* (Kali Theatre Tour). Recent/current projects: *Bobby and Amy* (Vault Festival & Pleasance, Edinburgh), *This Island's Mine* (Kings Head Theatre May 2019), *Forge* (R&D throughout 2019 with Rachel Mars), *Holocaust Brunch* (BAC, JW3, Arts Depot, throughout 2019), *The Faun Project* and *Desperate Gestures* (With choreographer Joseph Mercier throughout 2019), Community projects with The Egg & Kiln (Jan - Dec 2019), *Your Sexts are Shit* (Rachel Mars,

Summerhall, Touring 2019), *The Soothing Presence of Strangers* (Audio piece with Rhiannon Armstrong, London Borough of Culture 2019). www.dinahmullen.com

Jessica Thanki – Tour Stage Manager

With a BA in Theatre Production, Jessica has been stage managing for the last 10 years on an array of productions, including: *Maybe Father* (Talawa/Young Vic); *Behna* (Kali/Birmingham Rep); *It Hasn't Happened Yet* (Liz Carr, Tour); *Squid* (Theatre Royal Stratford East, Tour); *Brixton Rocks* (Tara Arts, Tour); *Tagore's Women* (Kali/Southwark Playhouse); *Sports Play* (Just a Must, UK and International Tour); *Dea* by Edward Bond (Sutton Theatres); *Now You See Me, Now You Don't* (Immediate Theatre, Tour); *The Ruck* (Lawrence Batley Theatre, Tour); *Tales of Birbal* (Mashi, Tour); *Typhoon* (Yellow Earth, Soho/Rich Mix); *Clockwork Canaries* (TRP, The Drum); *Cathy* (Cardboard Citizens, Tour); *Inside Bitch R&D*, (Clean Break, Royal Court); *Broken Dreams* (Kestrel, Royal Court); *Gentle Giant* (Bamboozle, Melbourne); *Muddy Choir* (Theatre Centre, Tour); *We're Going on a Bear Hunt* (KWFE UK and International Tour).

Chris Grogan – Assistant Stage Manager

During the winter months Chris dusts off his ASM hat and once again tiptoes about backstage. He's worked on many shows over the past 12 years both on and off stage. He has many strings to his bow including dancing, acting, singing and being a magician. In downtime in the summer months he runs his own tour guiding company in London. If you see a man wandering the streets of London looking up curiously with amazement, chances are you have caught a glance of him.

Homing Birds

The seeds of the story and the characters arose out of a Kali Inspirations evening designed by the director, Helena Bell, for Kali's more established writers. The theme was 'War'. Despite our awareness of their futility and destruction, wars do keep looming up on our horizon without fail. I wanted to write about it but my exploration led me deeper into yet more immediate concerns.

The provocateur on that night was a British-Afghan journalist, Nadene Ghouri, who has authored the biography of a leading Afghan politician, Fawzia Koofi. Nadene has also co-written the story of a child refugee, Gulwali Passarlay. Both their success stories were compelling and suggested the contours of my fictional protagonists in *Homing Birds,* namely, Saeed Khattak and Raabia Durrani. Their chance encounter in London sets the drama in motion.

As the play evolved into its present form, the war theme receded and it became a meditation on notions of home and belonging that endlessly haunt a settler's imagination. Through Saeed, we experience the demons and losses of dislocation, the paradox of belonging and un-belonging and the conflicting demands and richness of two worlds that continue to throb in a migrant's bloodstream side by side. He has no live links with his birth family, there is no one waiting for him in Kabul, yet, he feels the pull of his personal history. His search for roots drives him to seek out his sister.

Ironically, he discovers more about his past than he bargained for. His journey to Kabul gives him an insight into the structures of power, his first glimpse of violence and the taste of resistance. It reveals those iniquities of society that his rosy memories of an innocent past had obscured.

My connection with the work became deeper and more visceral as it grew into a play about displacement, albeit arising out of war. It charts the pain of separation and the subsequent search for moorings. Few of us stay rooted to a birthplace, most of us end up uprooting ourselves even if we have not been evicted brutally from a familiar setting.

We've all experienced moments of loss and absence that breed nostalgia and lead us to romanticising the past and erasing its worst injustices. *Homing Birds* shines a light on the shadows of memory reconstructed in absence. What I relished interrogating most was not so much the collateral damage caused by unnecessary wars imposed by a history of invasions but the deeper moral question of how to salvage human relationships in that hellish scenario... the depths of love and commitment that bind us to strangers.

It's been a remarkable journey of discovery, facilitated by my brilliant director, Helena Bell, my thoughtful and incisive dramaturge, Suzanne Bell and the talented actors who read the play for us through several drafts.

–Rukhsana Ahmad

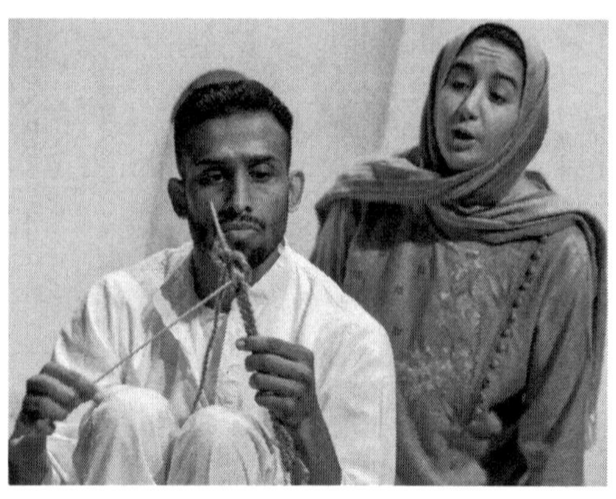

Jay Varsani and
Mona Khalili
Photo: Robert Day

HOMING BIRDS

Rukhsana Ahmad

The first performance of *Homing Birds* was in The Drum Studio at the Theatre Royal Plymouth on 9 October 2019.

Directed by Helena Bell.

CHARACTERS

Saeed Khattak – 24, British Afghan

Michael Davies – early 60's, white, Saeed's adoptive father

Raabia Durrani – 35, Afghan politician

Nazneen Khattak (Ekram) – 27, Saeed's sister

Setting:

London and Kabul. Today.

NOTES:

/ Indicates an interruption in the dialogue.

For this production: Soundtrack news footage courtesy of Al Jazeera (http://blip.tv/file/528100)

Excerpts from speech by Karyn McCluskey at an Open University Open Minds Talk on 18 May 2016 (http://www.open.ac.uk/research)

SCENE ONE

The stage is in darkness. Slowly a spot profiles Saeed, centre stage, in white.

We hear the sound of birds flapping. Pigeons cooing .

He turns to audience.

SAEED   The trick is never to dwell on a nightmare. Instead, you fetch up a good memory from the ragbag that's your head.

'Go and talk to your pigeons,' Baba would say, when we got bored. He taught us pigeon language while we watched him feed them, clean out their coops, set them free to fly every day then lure them back home by twilight.

Nazneen and I sat by the birds all afternoon watching them wooing and clucking, their heads wrapped round their mates' necks. Not a worry in the world, no cares, no fear of death, no sense of its meaning.

Now, it's ever at my door.

When I was seven, I watched them bury my brother, Zafar. They laid him, on a shelf dug into the side of the grave, like a book laid flat on its side. Someone said a prayer and they started shovelling mud into the hole. It took forever to fill. A centipede was crawling in and out of the mud ...and tiny brown ants, the kind that bite. I howled, I begged them to stop. No one listened to me. All around me I could see grown men weeping.

Friends brought food that night and sat Nazneen and me down to feed us. Only Moray wouldn't stop crying, couldn't eat a thing. No mother could... not on the first day...

'Zafar is in heaven,' Baba told us, when he came in to check on us last thing at night, 'in that evergreen garden with rivers of milk and honey, where your father lives, with all the martyrs. They will live forever.' He never mentioned death. No one did.

But when Keetu died, right in front of me, I saw it for real. At the Hungarian border. We were all terrified of being grilled on the barbed wire – no one warned us about the snipers. I never saw who fired the shot that split his skull. He was only 15, but he took good care of me; made me feel safe. All through the journey, he joked and clowned to make us all laugh, until that awful moment – when he turned into a fucking nightmare...

Enter Michael. Switches on a light.

MICHAEL   Nightmare, isn't it? Glasses all over the damn house. Didn't know we had so many friends!

SAEED   Mostly hers.

MICHAEL   The last two looked as if they were never leaving – the young woman in white with the ridiculously tall man. Afghan, right?

SAEED   Croatian. Mum knew them all by name.

MICHAEL   Sorry. I never recognised anyone from your network!

MICHAEL   Nightcap?

SAEED   Not for me, thanks.

MICHAEL   Not even a camomile tea?

Michael switches the radio on.

SAEED   Not right now, Michael.

MICHAEL   It's only Radio 4. Gets too quiet, by yourself/

SAEED   Please?

Michael switches it off.

SAEED   Thanks.

MICHAEL *(hovers)* Glad it's over. Went off okay, don't you think?

SAEED   Except... the serviettes...

MICHAEL   Yep. Forgot those. And we ran out of red wine... Not good. *(Beat)* She'd have hated all our cock-ups. Every birthday party, she found a new theme. Cake, candles, décor, everything toned in perfectly/

SAEED   Hmm...

MICHAEL   The only birthday memory she ever got out of you was the Prophet's birthday. Am I right?

SAEED   We weren't the kind of family that does birthdays. We celebrated that and Eid every year though ...

MICHAEL   There was a half-eaten spring roll in Jenny's favourite vase.

SAEED   Weird! Hope it wasn't one of the Afghans?

MICHAEL   Who knows. Can you blame them? The canapés were dreadful ... Weren't they?

Pause.

SAEED   You don't light a fire/

MICHAEL   What?

SAEED   In the house of death. First three days ... you don't cook.

MICHAEL   Makes sense. Choosing canapés was the last thing I felt like doing. If only she'd had the chance to plan things...

Pause.

SAEED   She might've chosen wicker over a cardboard coffin.

MICHAEL   Do you think...?

Pause.

SAEED   I can tidy up here, Michael. You sit down and enjoy your whiskey.

Michael sits. Saeed turns up his music. Michael sits up to listen.

MICHAEL   Haven't heard that Leonard Cohen song in years. Where did you find it?

Saeed turns it off.

SAEED   In Mum's car – along with some Rai and Afghan music/

MICHAEL   She was... pretty special. Wasn't she?

SAEED   Hmm...

MICHAEL   Remind me to play it at her memorial service, won't you?

SAEED   Written on my heart! I'll never forget Mum's words, her cautions, recipes, stories... none of them were lost in the fire.

MICHAEL   –

SAEED   I didn't know... she ... asked for a cremation/

MICHAEL   We never discussed funeral plans. You know how it was... *(Beat)* It's the most ethical way – even if it was, maybe a tad insensitive not to warn you?

SAEED   No worries. Who am I to complain?

MICHAEL   I didn't think. I guess, she would've consulted you/

SAEED   And I'd have a grave - to mark my loss. Somewhere, to visit. Who knows if I'll find any for the rest of them in Kabul...

MICHAEL   Sorry! For what it's worth... *(Beat)* Committals are never easy, anyway. *(Beat)* Surely time will heal? Everyone kept telling me that today.

Exit Michael. Saeed sits.

SCENE TWO

Saaed recalls a scene from the past. Enter Nazneen. Spreads a sheet, lights incense. She covers her head solemnly and recites.

NAZNEEN   Inna lilla hay wa inna elahi raajey-oon

'From God we come, and unto Him we shall return...'

SAEED   Nazneen, what if Zafar went up to heaven and found no one there?

NAZNEEN   Hush...Saeed, don't be silly! Allah's up there...and/

SAEED   So what does he look like?

NAZNEEN   Like Baba: very old with a long white beard, except His face is shiny and it glows. He wears long white robes, like the Arabs.

SAEED   I don't believe you.

NAZNEEN   You'll end up in hell with all the communists, if you don't –

SAEED   Communists? What are they?

NAZNEEN   Bad people. Years ago, they came to conquer Afghanistan. Baba and his friends fought them and saved us from evil.

SAEED   Allah doesn't look like Baba. Baba told me he's not like anybody we know. I think he's a…a huge football of silver light, colour of the moon. He has eyes all over him – so he sees everything

NAZNEEN   You're silly. And you talk too much you know. Don't ask Moray about Zafar again. It upsets her… Okay?

SAEED   But I miss him… When's he coming back, Nazneen?

NAZNEEN   Ask Baba. What do I know…? *(Beat)* Saeed? You upset, Saadi? Hey… look! Look what I found!

SAEED   That's mine! Baba gave it to me for Afsar – I swear

NAZNEEN   Yours was just blue and white.

NAZNEEN   Look, red stones, then green, then blue. It's a girly one? He bought it for Veena/

SAEED   Veena?

NAZNEEN   The little brown pigeon he bought for me – she flew off one day and never came back. Baba got this to cheer me up. 'Don't give up hope,' he said, 'one day she'll find her way home, all by herself'.

SAEED   So where's mine? I know I had one too...

NAZNEEN   Look after your stuff. Ask Moray – maybe she knows.

SAEED   Nazneen? Can I have this? Just to hold it for a bit?

NAZNEEN   But don't you dare lose it, Saadi! Only for a bit – but not forever. Okay?

Exit Nazneen.

SCENE THREE

Front room. Enter Saeed, dressed in a traditional afghan coat. He puts his hands in the pocket and brings out a bracelet, spins it in his hands. It falls to the floor. He picks it up, pockets it again.

Enter Michael, clutching the guardian under his arm.

MICHAEL   Going somewhere interesting?

SAEED   A reception Mum and I were invited to.

MICHAEL   Reception? Sounds... posh.

SAEED   Could be... the charity's in Kensington.

MICHAEL   You're representing your network, I take it?

SAEED   Will try to.

MICHAEL   Good. You'll be fine. You mustn't let it go.

SAEED   They won't let me go – I think. Anyway, I can't ever stop being an Afghan, can I?

MICHAEL   Um. Might be easier if you became more of a Brit?

SAEED   Is it an either/or for me, then ...?

MICHAEL   Reckon we'll find out, in the fullness of time.

Hangs up the coat on a hanger.

SAEED   And you? Any plans for tonight?

MICHAEL   Plenty of options. Got the TV guide and some Netflix picks

SAEED   Why don't you come with me? Let's make a new team –

MICHAEL   Pretend to be Jenny? Receptions aren't my scene. Standing around with a glass, jabbering about nothing in particular isn't conversing.

SAEED   Hunkering in here for two full weeks isn't you either.

MICHAEL   I'm working on a routine, Saeed. Don't worry about me.

Saeed takes the coat off and starts folding it. Michael flips the remote.

24Hr news blares a report about a bombing in Kabul.

MICHAEL   There we go again.

Saeed listens for a few seconds.

SAEED   Ugh – the same bulletin. Can't bear it!

Gunshots on TV. Michael watches him and turns it off.

MICHAEL   The violence, you mean? *(Saeed shrugs)* What's the reception in aid of?

SAEED   The Afghan Minister for Education is being awarded. Now Mum would've bonded with her by the end of the evening.

MICHAEL   It's a woman?

SAEED   Yes. Surprise, surprise.

MICHAEL   Remarkable! In a good way. Why would you befriend a politician tho'? Scum of the earth.

SAEED   Mostly, yes, but some are useful. Anyway, they can't all be bad. Mum always petitioned local MPs for our asylum cases.

MICHAEL   And who wants to take asylum in Afghanistan, Saeed?

SAEED   I got more than asylum when you and Mum took me in: a whole new life and a new family out here – But I won't have you jeer at Afghans or, Afghanistan.

MICHAEL   Och, I'm not jeering, Saeed, just curious why we need to befriend an Afghan politician. You're always criticising the government yourself.

Pause.

MICHAEL   A minute ago, you couldn't even bear to watch on TV what's going on out there.

SAEED   The tone of the coverage bothers me. Cold and... distancing.

He takes the bracelet from his pocket and fiddles with it.

MICHAEL   Hey. I thought you'd stopped carrying that bit of jewellery around?

SAEED   Found it in the pocket of this coat. I'll leave it at home – don't want to lose it.

Saeed puts it on a table.

MICHAEL   Might come in handy for breeding pigeons in London Zone 2.

SAEED   Ha bloody ha! It's a keepsake from happy days in Ghazni. A memento of my brave white Afsar.

MICHAEL   Memento? I like that word, though I'm not sure what qualifies: a mug, or a favourite scarf of hers?

Pause.

SAEED   Michael? Just come with me today – It will help me break the ice with this politician. She's bound to like you: you're white and you've got this gravitas thing...

MICHAEL   Nonsense! I feel like a traitor, going without Jenny. Going instead of her, makes me feel even worse.

SAEED   I like parties but I hate walking into the room alone.../

MICHAEL   ...Um...that's normal/

SAEED   She'd want you to go. We'll leave early. I usually do.

Pause.

MICHAEL   And you can spare one of those jackets for me?

SAEED   Are you serious? You want to wear a chapan?

MICHAEL   Is that what you call it in Pashto?

SAEED   Could be: Pashto, Dari? Or neither? I'm not an Afghan specialist... It's an Uzbeki garment, I believe.

MICHAEL   And Karzai used it to concoct a national outfit of sorts...

SAEED   Mind you, Baba had one like this. He'd often tell Nazneen: 'Your grandma made it for me. Every stitch knitted with love.'

MICHAEL   So there was a germ of truth in it?

SAEED   We're likely to find out more about the country if we attend. No?

MICHAEL   I don't trust politicians. Certainly not those who try to sell state nationalism. He looked good in it, though. (*Beat*) Didn't Tom Ford call him the chicest man on the planet?

SAEED   Yeah... what a dickhead! As if chic is all you need to run a country caught up in a civil war... (*Beat*) No, Michael. I definitely don't have a spare one of those. Pick something less exotic: a floral red and green cravat with a dark evening suit will definitely catch her eye.

MICHAEL   A blazer and tie is my best offer –

Saeed gives him a nod. Exit Michael, shaking his head.

Lights dim.

SCENE FOUR

Saaed recalls a scene from the past.

Enter Nazneen.

NAZNEEN   It's not easy, I swear. And boys don't knit. Ever seen one doing it?

SAEED   Can if they want to. Who says they can't?

NAZNEEN   Baba says. I'll teach you, but he'll be cross if he finds out.

She pulls out wool and a pair of knitting needles from her bag. Sits close to him, cross-legged.

SAEED   We won't let him see it, until it's done. Yes?

NAZNEEN   Right. Hold the needles up like this, make a loop and go through it – that's plain – if you come up the loop from below, it's purl... do first row plain second purl and you get this simple pattern. Want to try? Don't pull it too tight. Ruins the shape.

SAEED   Okay. I'll be careful.

Saeed struggles with the needles and wool.

SAEED   It's hard. What's it going to be?

NAZNEEN   A scarf for you, of course. Who else? For your big trip. Every stitch knitted with love... Baba's pet – Maa's precious son! They spoil you – between them.

SAEED   Me? Spoilt? How?

NAZNEEN   He takes you wherever he goes. Maa won't feed me until you've eaten/

SAEED   Where does he take me? To funerals, Friday prayers and the market. All full of old men; no one my age. It's no fun at all.

NAZNEEN   He didn't let me go to Zafar's funeral. All I wanted to do was to hold his hand. To comfort him, be near him.

SAEED   He had no hands/

NAZNEEN   What? Don't lie to me!

SAEED   I swear to you – I never saw his hands. He was all wrapped up in a white sheet - like a bed-roll...

NAZNEEN   Saeed – don't you even know how they wrap a shroud? Arms by your side, palms open. You come empty-handed and you leave empty-handed...

SCENE FIVE

At a reception. Gentle Afghan music plays in the background.

RAABIA   Fourteen or fifteen years? That's a generation...

Saeed counts on his fingers.

SAEED   Feels like a lifetime. Yet, some things are so vivid in my memory, I can almost touch them.

RAABIA   Far too long to be away from your mother country, Dr. Davies. Memory begins to fade after six months.

SAEED   Call me Saeed, please. I prefer it.

RAABIA   Saeed? Hmm. Happiness – great name they gave you!

SAEED   Sa'eed. You say it exactly as Moray used to. One day, I hope I'll find the happiness she dreamed of, for me...

RAABIA   A young doctor, working in London – it's a good life! You should be happy already. Aren't you?

SAEED   Should be happy? Are you?

RAABIA   Um, I believe I am – happy with the choices I've made so far. But people change, Saeed, and so do places. If true blue Afghans returned home they'd discover the new Afghanistan. Visit this autumn: it's a good time. Be our guest.

SAEED   Thanks... for your kind invitation!

RAABIA   I mean it. We need you. Our country needs you just as much as it needs me.

SAEED   Michael! You've got to hear this...

He waves to Michael who approaches, hand extended.

Raabia hesitates, greets him hand on heart.

MICHAEL   Michael Davies – delighted to meet you. I loved the tone of your speech; formal yet friendly. Nothing high and mighty in it.

RAABIA   So kind of you, Mr. Davies! Thank you. Honoured to meet your dad, Saeed.

MICHAEL   Sadly, it's just the two of us now...

RAABIA   Sincere condolences. Awful when people are snatched out of our lives abruptly. God and His mysterious ways/

MICHAEL   Indeed.

SAEED   We forget how precarious life is.

RAABIA   As a doctor, you're probably much more aware of it.

SAEED   I was no use as a doctor, when it happened. All I could do for Mum was to recognise the stroke...

MICHAEL   You helped, Saeed.

SAEED   There came a point we had to accept defeat.

RAABIA   I admire that ability. I wish I was better at it. I do the opposite, dig in – vow to fight my corner/

MICHAEL   That explains your success – which we're celebrating today.

RAABIA   I feel very lucky and blessed... It's great to get an award and recognition for work that I love.

SAEED   Baba called it Kismet.

RAABIA   O yes! She's been a good friend so far. And please don't let her turn against me, Ya Allah; she's the worst enemy possible.

MICHAEL   Now that's fatalism, isn't it? It discourages human effort.

SAEED   We're not talking prep for school exams, Michael, just random bad luck – like lightning picking a house to strike.

RAABIA   Exactly, we've all met with luck, both good and bad.

MICHAEL   Hard to deny misfortune, but I think you can always counter it.

SAEED   We can? Random bad luck? Like a bomb deflecting to your house, or a plane crashing on a bridge ... all that shit from hell that hits ordinary people's lives – out of the blue.

RAABIA   Hard to know the right answers. Yet we all think we know.

Michael takes a glass of wine from the table.

MICHAEL   Luckily, ordinary citizens don't have to pretend to know them. *(Beat)* You don't mind if I...?

RAABIA   Not at all. You know foreigners can buy drinks in Afghanistan, so you won't need to worry about it.

SAEED   I don't drink. Mum encouraged me not to...

MICHAEL   Jenny was particular about raising Saeed to respect his faith –

RAABIA   I'm glad she did that.

Michael looks at Saeed uncertainly.

SAEED   I've no memory of my father but I was taught to stand by his faith.

MICHAEL   More or less the case with me too...

RAABIA   It seems you, Saeed, and I, do have something in common:. I never knew my father either.

MICHAEL   What a sorry club we make – the three of us. Seems wrong to hi-five on it though...

RAABIA   Quite! We won't. We've all survived without them –

MICHAEL   Thrived without them, perhaps?

RAABIA   Oooh, careful, sir! Once I foolishly tweeted: 'It's the mothers who watch over children when God forgets to look,' and got a bunch of extremists baying for my blood.

MICHAEL   Goodness me! Why?

RAABIA   Blasphemer, they said. "Allah never forgets anything..." And: "How can mothers be better than Allah?"

MICHAEL   It's tough to be constantly in the public eye.

RAABIA   Indeed.

SAEED   True – we all survived... But so sad that every second Afghan I meet has lost their father in the war?

RAABIA   I didn't. Mine's a long story. I'll tell you when you visit Kabul.

MICHAEL   Kabul? Who's going to Kabul? You're not going! Are you, Saeed?

SAEED   Hmm... not this week, of course... or the next...

RAABIA   Make a plan. You must come, even if it's only for a visit/

MICHAEL   Kabul is always in the news...

RAABIA   There's no need for alarm, Mr. Davies. We live there, many millions of us. It's just fine.

SAEED   I'm sure you're right. But if I choose to come with Medicins Sans Frontieres, I'm afraid they'll send me where I'm needed.

RAABIA   Avoid Kunduz. That's where the heavy fighting is... I can swing that for you. 'Specially if I do get the portfolio for health.

MICHAEL   Enter a war zone and you multiply the odds against yourself tenfold. It's dangerous, really.

RAABIA   We're not in a war zone – war on terror is different. It's assymetrical –

MICHAEL   Maybe. But it's just as lethal...

SAEED   I'll be in a hospital, Michael, not in a frontline trench!

MICHAEL   Symmetrical or not, an improvised bomb kills as surely as a traditional weapon...

RAABIA   We're living through it all, sir... More Afghans die out there than any other nationality.

MICHAEL   Exactly my point – it's not a safe destination.

RAABIA In a sense, nowhere is safe. You've had terror attacks in London and Manchester too. And a member of your parliament was murdered in her own constituency. Right? We'll look after you, Saeed. Mr. Davies, peace is our goal, and we need the ablest and brightest Afghans to return and help rebuild the country.

MICHAEL It's... it's... just too soon for Saeed. After this trauma/

SAEED Mmm... Lucky I met you today, Mrs. Durrani. For ages I've been thinking about reconnecting with Afghanistan.

RAABIA It's a great time in Afghanistan. We're transitioning as a country. Moving steadlily towards democracy. Art and culture are thriving/

MICHAEL But those terrorist attacks are worse now. Don't you agree?

RAABIA Let's keep them in perspective, Kabul is safe. We were ravaged by war but we're a young country, keen to modernise. More women in parliament, in the arts, in banks, and businesses... than ever before. We need you, all of you.

MICHAEL Glass of wine?

RAABIA O no, thanks! I don't drink. Not even in private. Good Muslim, like our charming Afghan doctor here. Can't afford not to be.

MICHAEL Real gem, our Saeed. We were so lucky to have found him.

RAABIA Your peace lures our young away. We've lost big time; millions died in the wars and millions fled.

Long pause.

SAEED   Like I did, I had to... Michael and Mum helped me deal with that awful journey.

RAABIA   I've heard terrible stories about it.

SAEED   Every night I cursed Moray for sending me away. I wouldn't talk to her on the phone even after we got here.

RAABIA   But she did it to protect you! Hope you call her regularly now?

SAEED   Mum tried to get me to speak to Moray. I might've done. But, by the time I got round to it... Seems I do have a knack for losing my nearest/

RAABIA   Who can fight God's will? Moray would be so proud to see you now, a qualified doctor, returning to help your country. No one wants refugees these days – least of all, Afghan asylum seekers/

SAEED   Mrs. Durrani, of course, Michael doesn't think like that!

MICHAEL   Hold on, Saeed. You don't need to defend me –

RAABIA   I'm sure you're different, sir.

MICHAEL   Hey... let's not talk about me... Tell us about your amazing work for women's education.

RAABIA   Girls are still herded into marriage everywhere, but for Afghan women, it's worse. I've always fought for their education. It's the only route to justice and survival.

SAEED   Exactly what Mum used to say.

RAABIA   My mother learnt this the hard way. After her divorce, she got a tiny income teaching children how to read the Qura'n. *(Turns to Michael)* I'm determined to serve Afghan women. If they're held back by their own faith, I have to challenge them; but I do it subtly.

SAEED   Mum would have loved you, Mrs. Durrani.

RAABIA   Hate to admit it, but the invasion has benefited Afghan women. We got some space, some rights. As for Kabul, you won't recognise it; it's all changed.

SAEED   That's exciting. I can't wait to visit, to see it for myself... *(Beat)* What I remember best is our kitchen in the courtyard. Every morning I'd wake up and see Moray working there. I'd sit by her feet and my sister would fetch me hot milk and sugared almonds...

RAABIA   Mmm. I love sugared almonds with green tea. We lost so much in the war but not those, thank God. So much has changed though – US troops cleared the mines laid by the Taliban, levelled the homes they'd bombed themselves, and built a huge American University in Kabul. We're all proud of Kabul-e-Nau: gleaming and bright. You'll love it.

SAEED   Is that where you live now? Near the campus?

RAABIA   No, no. We're in a fine district right in the centre: the safest zone. An Italian architect designed and built our house for us.

MICHAEL   They've got an eye for design, the Italians...

RAABIA   I wish my father could see it. I've heard it's the envy of the richest man in his tribe ...

SAEED   Respect. Maybe he does see it? Who's to say he can't?

RAABIA   I hope so.

Raabia pulls out a visiting card and hands it to Saeed.

He takes it, reads it then puts it away carefully.

SAEED   Thank you. I'd love to visit just to see your house one day.

RAABIA   Inshallah. If you need my help to get there, just call me.

SAEED   Fantastic. I will.

Raabia bows. Saeed and Michael respond. Raabia exits.

Michael stretches out his hand for her card.

MICHAEL   Bit of a self-promoter, isn't she? All these abbreviations! Honorary degrees I presume, not fake ones?

SAEED   You've got to hand it to her. She is a star. To be fair, she's promoting the country, not herself.

MICHAEL   She's playing you, Saeed. Paints a rosy picture. We know everyone in Kabul is exposed to danger, except the elite.

SAEED   I'd like to go and put it to the test/

MICHAEL   And your Fellowship exam?

SAEED   I'll take it when I'm back. I'm not ready yet. I'll cover the fee.

MICHAEL   And what's that I heard you say about Medicins Sans Frontieres? You never even told me you were considering them...

SAEED   I told Mum.

MICHAEL   When? On her death bed – when she couldn't speak to me?

SAEED   Michael –

MICHAEL   She'll never forgive me, if you come to any harm/

SAEED   Heavens, Michael, cool it. You heard Mrs. Durrani just now/

MICHAEL   If I were you, Saeed, I'd take her with a pinch of salt. She's a politician not a saint by any stretch of the imagination

SAEED   Because she's a politician, or, because she's an Afghan?

MICHAEL   Are you serious? What are you suggesting?

Pause.

SAEED   Nothing. Forget I said that...

MICHAEL   And I'm the one who's been drinking?

SCENE SIX

Saaed recalls a scene from the past. He sits on the floor with a bowl of food.

SAEED   Is there any more sugar?

NAZNEEN   It's sweet enough.

SAEED   No...it's not. Does Moray love me as much as she loved Zafar and you??

NAZNEEN   Of course she does...

SAEED   Then why do I have to go and not you?

NAZNEEN   Because you're a boy.

SAEED   So?

NAZNEEN   Boys are more special -

SAEED   But you always say they're not.

NAZNEEN   They are – in some ways

SAEED   How?

NAZNEEN   Girls have to change their names when they get married. Because you're a boy you carry Baba's name, your son will carry your name and then his son – that way the family name lives on and on and on.

SAEED   It goes: Khattak, Khattak, Khattak, Khattak forever...

They start giggling.

NAZNEEN   Till you come to a stop.

SAEED   Like, if I die without having a son, the way Zafar died?

NAZNEEN   God forbid. Don't talk of sad things first thing in the morning.

SAEED   You started it...

NAZNEEN   You did! *(Calling)* Moray... Saeed's not eating his breakfast.

SAEED   I don't want to go without you, Naz. Why have I got to go?

NAZNEEN   Hush... Listen to that... can you hear the pigeons cooing?

SAEED   Yes. I can. Haven't they been fed today?

NAZNEEN   Listen to them... and maybe you can tell what they say?

SAEED   I know what they're saying: more sugar, more sugar, more sugar. I said: it's not sweet enough.

NAZNEEN   It's fine.

Nazneen rises, takes the bowl and exits. Saeed starts packing a suitcase.

SCENE SEVEN

At the airport. Saeed arrives with his case.

Enter Michael, sends a text and waits,

Saeed pulls his mobile out to read a text.

Michael, looks at his watch. Then cranes his neck, scanning the crowd.

Saeed rushes forward to meet him, Michael holds up his palms.

MICHAEL   Didn't mean to alarm you.

SAEED   Scared the shit out of me! I know you hate airports.

Michael pulls out the bracelet from his pocket.

SAEED   Can't believe I forgot that. It's like a talisman, thank you. Owe you one, Michael.

MICHAEL   It's not a big deal...

SAEED   Just the kind of thing Mum used to do.

MICHAEL   Maybe she's pulling the strings up there somewhere...

SAEED   Thanks, Mum, if it's still you... Seriously, thanks, Michael.

MICHAEL   Coffee?

SAEED   Don't wanna miss my flight. Let's just hang out for a few/

MICHAEL   ...moments of free parental advice.

SAEED   It's a familiar hazard – have risked it before.

MICHAEL   In one ear, out the other, typically unheeded, un-needed –

SAEED   Ten seconds to go.

MICHAEL   Seek her help – but only if there's no choice. She's a politician – they're self-serving, as a rule.

SAEED   That's unfair, Michael! I can't think of anything I could possibly do for her in return.

MICHAEL   Exactly. What's up her sleeve?

SAEED   I've no known family or tribe to help. What choice do I have?

MICHAEL   Sure....

SAEED   I'll try her. I know it's a big ask and she may not help

MICHAEL   I know you need to find your sister, Saeed, but be discreet.

SAEED   Don't worry! Thanks for fetching this–

MICHAEL   No worries. Best to hang on to your good luck charms.

SAEED   Got to go now/

MICHAEL   Keep a low profile. No hero stuff. No arguments. Stay cool.

SAEED   I'm always careful. You guys turned me into a real wimp.

MICHAEL   We're all works in progress. You turn a page when you return, but do stay wimpish out there.

SAEED   Will do my wimpish best.

MICHAEL   If you come back loud and aggressive, I'll surprise you with a make-over at 65. Red hair, orange trousers, psychedelic sunglasses...

SAEED   No, Michael! Let's not. You're fine, just as you are.

MICHAEL   Thanks, mate! Go carefully, Saeed... Safe travels. *(Beat)* Send us a text when you get there. Or two...

SCENE EIGHT

Choreographed movement scene at the airport. Transition to Kabul. With a new soundscape, noise and Afghan music.

SCENE NINE

Kabul. Day.

SAEED *(to audience)*

It took us thirteen months to get to London. Getting to Kabul in ten hours was such a doddle. Forget sleep, I was too excited to read or even to watch a film...

I burst out of the plane and stood on the tarmac blinking in the sun, wondering if I should kiss the ground, like the Pope; but fellow Afghans rushed around, jostling me, infecting me with their haste.

I looked up at the sky. Magic – the perfect blue I remembered. The sunlight was sharp as polished steel, the kind you never see in London. Before the day was out, I was at Bagh-e-Babur. What a fucking shock that was: all shiny new buildings and manicured gardens. So fake!

I needed to get closer to our house in Kabul, to see it for real. I'd dreamt of it so often but I'd no idea how to get there. I looked for the old alleyways. They'd vanished. All gone. Mrs. Durrani would likely dismiss it as collateral damage. On my first day back in Kabul, it was painful. Not a single house remained: no familiar faces, no landmarks.

Until that moment, I was really excited about coming home. I felt Nazneen was close by me, I wondered if she was there, if she could see me. She was older, so she'd know me; wouldn't she? ... I asked passers-by if they knew where people had moved to when the houses were pulled down, but they didn't... No one knew. No one cared.

Baba told me I had to go just one day before I was due to leave. Moray, never prepared me for the journey. Late that night, she heard me sobbing and came in. She took me into her own bed. All night, she kept hugging me, her palm stroking my back as she prayed and blew warm prayer breath over my forehead and hair. 'Go to sleep, son,' she said. ' I'll join you before long, inshallah'. She never came...' *(He pulls a sweet out of a paper bag of sweets.)*

The world has changed but these haven't! Couldn't resist them: orange and lime-green segments exactly like the sweets Baba got us from the shack in Ghazni. Nazneen loved the tangerines; my favourites were lemon and lime, so tart they almost ripped your tongue. (*He tries to hum. Echoes of: "an Afghan song/music"*) Crazy. To come miles away from the home I love to remember boiled sweets and old songs.

SCENE TEN

In the MSF hospital ward. Sound of a wooden flute. The simple melody fades.

Enter Nazneen.

NAZNEEN *(to audience)*

Out here, in the hospital where I work, it must annoy the patients and maybe the staff too.... But it's a romantic sound – when you hear it at night across the hills and valleys. You can almost hear a lover sending a coded message to his beloved, like that Hindu god – was it Rama or Krishna?

The day my husband died, I started thinking about life and its meaning... Years ago, he took me to see a Hindi film. The heroine dies but is reborn and returns to marry the hero again. Ekram turned to me and smiled: 'Now that's a gift, wife, isn't it? Another life on this earth with someone you love.'

Huh... love? I thought.

It's a strange idea. I said to him. Not love, rebirth, hmm? Yes, he said. And you earn it, only if you're perfect. If you're not, you return as a lower life form: a dog, or a toad maybe.

Ekram was a good man but you couldn't accuse him of being perfect. For a time, I wondered if he was the koel singing in our pomegranate tree. I tried to spot him amongst the leaves, maybe he's come to say, 'Greetings, Wife. I'm back. Here again to help you.'

What if he returned as a younger more handsome version of himself? Mmm…

But the nightingale vanished that summer, and I got no more messages from the other world. Life with Ekram was never easy but things got so much harder after his death.

Who would fear death, if it always took you up another rung or two of the ladder? I started dreaming of other lives I'd choose if I could. Not a doctor's life, that's too hard. I dream of returning as the Queen of Persia, or, the King of Bhutan, or, even the President of the US. Not because I'm hungry for power or glory but because I need the freedom from money worries. And maybe one could do things for others…? The problem is: perfection is impossible. It's hard, so hard to be alone all the time.

And it's impossible to be good all the time…

Knock on the door. Enter Saeed.

NAZNEEN   Doctor?

SAEED   Sorry to barge in – there's never a quiet moment to catch you. Mrs. Ekram, isn't it? Am I saying it right?

NAZNEEN   It's fine, sir.

SAEED   It's about a patient in the men's general ward – the one in the yellow jumper – I see him alone mostly, shuffling cards or playing the flute?

NAZNEEN   Mansoor?

SAEED He rushes off whenever I greet him. But he seems relaxed around you, so ... I ... I wondered/

NAZNEEN He knows me. He's from Ekram's village.

SAEED A bit of a fixture, here. Right? I've given him two weeks. But he won't engage. What's his name again?

NAZNEEN Mansoor. He can't talk any more. Best to say – he won't talk – because the doctors can't find anything wrong with him.

SAEED And he uses the flute to communicate?

NAZNEEN I know him well so I pick up his meaning – if I focus on the notes he's playing...

SAEED Amazing.

NAZNEEN He writes down odd words, sometimes he uses traditional signs, if his meaning is too complicated.

SAEED What happened to him?

NAZNEEN He was injured in a bombing incident.

SAEED Recently?

NAZNEEN Not very recently... He lost his voice. I lost my husband. Now we share an anniversary, a history.

He steps back.

SAEED I'm so sorry. You're far too young to be a widow. I didn't know.

NAZNEEN I don't wear pure white or all black. Best to keep it quiet, to avoid the sharks out here in the city!

An alarm sounds.

SAEED There it goes again... scares the life out of me.

NAZNEEN It's just a panic alarm – alerts us to a possible security breach.

SAEED   It panics me for real. I've some bad memories.

NAZNEEN Round here, everyone does, I'm afraid.

SAEED   Sorry – to be so ... pathetic/

NAZNEEN You'll get used to it. Often it's nothing serious.

F/X alarm announces all clear.

NAZNEEN That's the all clear now... You can come and talk things through with me, if you're worried.

Saeed raises his eyebrows.

SAEED   Physician, heal thyself, she says...

NAZNEEN *(smiles)* No, no, not quite like that...

SAEED   I'm fine, Mrs. Ekram, thanks very much!

NAZNEEN I'm sure you are.

SAEED   Just fine... I promise you

Exit Nazneen.

SCENE ELEVEN

Lights up with a bluish tinge. Saeed recalls a memory. He whispers, trying to wake Michael up.

MICHAEL   Can't sleep?

SAEED   Can we check on Bobo?

MICHAEL   Not now, Saeed. It's late. Can't be him. Must be the wind –

SAEED   Please, Michael?

MICHAEL   He's poorly but he's a hefty wood pigeon – he'll be fine.

SAEED   I don't want to bury it.

MICHAEL   We won't have to. I promise you, he's fine/

SAEED   –

MICHAEL   You know the routine. Just turn the lights on to shake off the nightmares. And read a book to calm down. *(Beat)* Only ten minutes, by the clock. Promise me? Good lad.

Black out.

SCENE TWELVE

Hospital ward. Nazneen is getting ready to leave.

Enter Saeed.

NAZNEEN   Doctor?

SAEED   I've found a psychiatrist for Mansoor.

NAZNEEN   Thanks! But I do know him and his condition. I don't need help supporting him. I believe he's improving – steadily.

SAEED   Your decision. I apologise, I didn't guess you're a therapist.

NAZNEEN   That's a grand title. I'm just a health worker. I support patients who are traumatised or depressed.

SAEED   I'd seen you on the ward so I assumed you were...

NAZNEEN   A nurse? Would've taken years to get a nurse's qualification. I was married off before I finished school.

SAEED   You did well to get into part-time work then.

NAZNEEN   I'm full-time actually. I know three languages. I'm in here only three days a week. The other two days I do community visits.

SAEED   Is it harder to manage them in their own setting?

NAZNEEN   No. I think it's easier to unpick the problem. I see only women.

SAEED   Victims of trauma?

NAZNEEN   All kinds, really. Right now I've one who's lost her family, one who got burnt and disfigured. That's tough, and two new mums. A child bride who can't cope with motherhood, and one's had two miscarriages: her body wasn't ready for pregnancy, but she blames herself!

SAEED   This is a hard country–

NAZNEEN   Specially for girls – marry a stranger, accept a new home, serve a new family, do all the work and also produce and raise children when you're still a child yourself/

SAEED   And not ready for it.

NAZNEEN   Never the top of the list anywhere, is it?

SAEED   No. It really isn't. Nor is the shortage of medicines/

A few notes of the flute can be heard.

SAEED   There he goes again. It's him, isn't it?

NAZNEEN   Hmm...

SAEED   You've really bonded with him, haven't you?

NAZNEEN   Hmm. Ekram's artificial leg kept getting sore. The only hospital in the district was the MSF unit in Kunduz. The day we got there he came running to greet us, to help.

SAEED   Is that where it happened? In Kunduz?

NAZNEEN   Yes. When the bombing started, he and Mansoor were sent to the basement. Ekram was dead when they found them; he died shielding the boy with his body. Mansoor, terrified and shell-shocked, had to be pulled out of his rigid arms.

SAEED   I – I don't know what to say...

NAZNEEN   Thousands of grim stories out here. Some worse than mine – when I'm lost for words I recite the Muslim prayer

SAEED   The one that's a sobering reminder of death?

NAZNEEN   Yes, but it's comforting too.

SAEED   Does Mansoor remember what happened?

Nazneen shrugs.

NAZNEEN   We'll know if he ever recovers his ability to talk... *(Beat)* Not that I need to know more about the past, Doctor! I'm still learning to forget.

SAEED   Sorry to stir it up for you.

NAZNEEN   Tell me, are you enjoying Afghanistan or, is it all too scary?

SAEED   Bit of both, to be honest. I love working here. I'm learning all the time but this, this fighting for resources all the time is exhausting... It's good to feel useful, to think you're making a difference...

NAZNEEN   Can we, ordinary citizens, make a difference?

SAEED   Of course we can... I'm working on an idea to help build bridges between this country and the UK.

NAZNEEN   I have loads of ideas but never the chance to work on them.

SAEED   Let's hear yours.

NAZNEEN   We should get someone to campaign against child marriages. Women's lives would change totally if we banned them.

SAEED   I know just the person who can push that campaign/

NAZNEEN   Who?

SAEED   Mrs. Durrani, Raabia Durrani.

NAZNEEN   The new Health Minister? You know her?

SAEED   I do. I've got to see her anyway. I will ask her.

NAZNEEN   I hear she takes the official line – the only way to get on in a man's world. Yes?

SAEED   You sound as sceptical as my Dad...

A sudden blackout.

SAEED   O MY GOD! What the–?/

NAZNEEN   Power failure, I think, Doctor.

He lights a match. Finds a candle.

SAEED   ... Let me try her, anyway?

NAZNEEN   Sure... I better go before the neighbours start gossiping.

SAEED   Would they really?

NAZNEEN   What else would they do, if they didn't? Take care, Doctor Davies.

SAEED   And you Mrs. Ekram. You teach me how to understand others...

SCENE THIRTEEN

Saeed recalls a memory. Michael and Saeed are in a park, feeding pigeons.

MICHAEL   What do you have to say for yourself? *(Beat)* A child, a friend of yours, gets a nose-bleed; another one's homework is ruined. They're both accusing you, Saeed...

Saeed turns away.

MICHAEL   Tell me what happened? Toby and Nikki are much younger boys -

SAEED   –

MICHAEL   Both their parents complained to the Head. How would you feel in their shoes?

SAEED   They – ganged up on me.

MICHAEL   You must report bullying, Saeed. They wind you up and you fall for it. They make you look bad, every time. We've got to break this reaction thing.

SAEED   I hate that school...

MICHAEL   Can we try to unpack that – a bit?

SAEED   –

MICHAEL   I know how tough it is getting used to a new environment. We did it, as kids, a few times. Maybe you feel singled out – left out even? But remember, we're all unique, everyone has feelings, we all get hurt. You can't take it out on the others.

Saeed tries to run away from him.

MICHAEL   Calm down, Saeed. *(He holds Saeed as he starts hyperventilating.)* Take a deep breath. *(Saeed takes a deep breath)* And another... *(Saeed takes a deep breath)* You're here to stay. I'll speak to the Head. Listen, my man, if you agree to apologise you won't get a penalty from Mum. Tell you what? We don't even need to tell her... How's that?

Saeed looks at Michael, relieved.

SAEED *(whispers)* Deal...

Michael puts his arm round Saeed, leads him to a seat.

SCENE FOURTEEN

An Afghan song plays in the background. Saeed pulls out a card from his wallet, studies it. Then joins Raabia in the spotlight – the 'lounge' of her home.

SAEED   Amazing house, Mrs. Durrani. The security arrangements are watertight. Didn't think I'd get in/

RAABIA   Hope the guards didn't hassle you?

SAEED   Not at all. It's all necessary.

RAABIA   Sadly, yes! Before we sit down... Mustafa, my husband is sorry he can't join us. A slip disc, I'm afraid! Now... green tea, black tea or something cold?

SAEED   I'm exhausted. A good coffee to keep me awake. Or, English breakfast tea, please.

RAABIA   I like a tinge of the flag in mine. Green – that's my normal order at this time of day.

Raabia rings bell.

SAEED   Nothing to beat our green tea.

RAABIA   That's the spirit, Saeed. Afghanistan is a very special place.

SAEED   I believe in it, totally. Even argued with Michael, at times. But soon as I came off the plane, they got to me. I kept thinking: 'Noisy, disorderly brutes. No one's willing to queue, or wait their turn.' Even cars, buses, carts ran higgledy piggledy on the road to the Babur Garden – and that was a big disappointment on my very first day!

RAABIA   What? You did the Bagh-e-Babur on your first day in Kabul? A serious tourist, aren't you?

SAEED   Awful, to become a tourist in your motherland! No? It's the only chance I got. The hospital's full on!

RAABIA   Glad you made it to the gardens, even if you didn't like them.

SAEED   Wasn't the gardens I went for – I went looking for my family.

RAABIA   Did they live round there?

SAEED   I think so. I wondered if you might be able to help? Been trying for a month to find them. I've found no clues at all.

RAABIA   For sure. I'll help – all I can…

SAEED   It was a shock to see the place. The American University is where our homes used to be. I couldn't imagine the end of an entire community. Gone. All of them! I expected to find a few leads, some people from the past. I found none at all.

RAABIA   Decimated. In thirty years of war we've lost millions of lives, thousands of homes, hundreds of villages…

SAEED   Doesn't the government keep records? Of compensation schemes, for example?

RAABIA   People died, people fled, or were driven away. No one could maintain records back then. This war is older than you, Saeed.

SAEED   Even so.

RAABIA   When the Allied Forces got here, they were terrified of anyone in a turban. They bombed areas suspected of protecting militants until they were routed. And the Taliban mined every inch of land they surrendered. Destroyed communities/

SAEED   Moray was alone the day our house was hit. Is there any hope of finding my sister?

RAABIA   There's always hope. The future is bursting with promise. *(Beat)* You're here now, Saeed! That's a good start.

SAEED   Where do I begin to look?

RAABIA   Let me have full names and addresses…

SAEED   I've one sibling who survived the invasion. Nazneen, my sister. She was married off. But I've no contact details for her/

RAABIA   Not even her husband's name?

SAEED   Baba told me on the phone, but I'm afraid I forgot.

RAABIA   Tough. But don't worry. We'll find a way to trace her… First, tell me, which hospital did you join?

SAEED   The MSF Hospital in the South. Thank you so much for getting me to Kabul. I felt the pull of helpful strings.

RAABIA   Don't mention it. Enjoying working with them I hope?

SAEED   Immensely! A fine team of dedicated doctors and staff. Ever ready to improvise and make do! Huge learning curve for me. Do come and meet them. You'll see why I think they're terrific.

RAABIA   I'd love to. Thanks. Might make a good photo op' for us?

SAEED   I'm talking to an Afghan computer geek from the US. We're building a database to link our doctors digitally to consultants in the UK – to talk them through latest treatments. I'll match up the right specialist for each case/

RAABIA   Not many British doctors come out here. They're too nervous.

SAEED   I can incentivise them to advise doctors here remotely about complex cases on Skype, What'sApp, Viber, whatever.

RAABIA   That would save lives, make a vast difference, I'm sure. Fantastic! I knew you'd be worth your weight in gold – you've proved my point. So important to get our young talent back.

SAEED   Thanks for having faith in me. All hypothetical so far.

RAABIA   It's a great idea. I can make it happen. Times are tough but we might even get some US sponsorship. Right?

SAEED   I don't know about funding or resources. I'm a worker in a white coat. Give me patients and I'll get them well again...

RAABIA   Great soundbite. You're so quotable, Saeed. I'll get our press office to profile this issue here and in the UK and this idea will become reality long before you return to England...

SAEED   If only I wanted to be a celebrity! But all I want is peace and order in my life and a happy ending to my search.

RAABIA   I understand your need to connect with family. I'll help, I swear. But we need young Afghans to come back here and team up with those of us who are ready to pull out into the twenty-first century.

SAEED   Careful what you wish for. There are all sorts in the Diaspora: not everyone who lives overseas is liberal or liberated.

RAABIA   Good point. Tell me what you think of Kabul now?

SAEED   The MSF team are committed to the hilt. But we've no infrastructure, no organisational support. And – I hate seeing under-age pregnancies. One of our counsellors wants to campaign against child marriages. I knew you'd help her so I promised I'd request you to take her under your wing.

RAABIA   Early marriages? A tough one. She has the right idea – it's a major, major issue for women. But, as a nation, the one we need to focus on right now, is the economy/

SAEED   I'm so sorry. I've already told her you'd support the cause.

RAABIA   I do, of course I do. I agree it's the single biggest obstacle to women's education, health and survival. But we've got to work out a strategy, a pitch, to avoid a backlash.

SAEED   Well, then, I probably raised her hopes too high. Will you please, at least, see her?

RAABIA   Of course I will.../

SAEED   And will you help find my family too, please?

RAABIA   Now, listen, Saeed. It's never easy to trace lost families. Nazneen is a popular name and you don't know the family or even tribe she married into...

SAEED   I wasn't here when she was married off. It was soon after/

RAABIA   As your counsellor says, it's always far too soon – for girls – specially in a war zone.

SAEED   She could be somewhere close by.

RAABIA   Hmm... do you remember the school she attended?

SAEED   No. It was close to our house.

RAABIA   Name? *(Beat)* Oh, what a pity!

SAEED   I've listed neighbours and friends I could muster from memory.

RAABIA   Leave that with me. I'll ask Mustafa, too, if it's okay? He'll be sorry to have missed you. He enjoys entertaining.

SAEED   I'd love to meet him when I bring Mrs. Ekram to meet you.

RAABIA   Who's she?

SAEED   My colleague, the counsellor.

RAABIA   That's a thought. Maybe?

SAEED   Would be good to meet her. *(Beat)* This killim on the floor keeps catching my eye. I feel I've seen that pattern somewhere before. A classic perhaps?

RAABIA   Could be... *(Beat)* Saeed, my press team will interview you about the dream of returning to the mother country. *(Pause)* Let's hope and pray we find your sister soon.

SAEED   Counting on you, Mrs. Durrani. I'm not good at prayers but I wish you the best.

Exit Saeed.

She lights a candle. Uses it to light another two.

RAABIA   I was the seventh daughter. My mother got no flowers, no gifts, no thanks for giving birth to me.

Instead, she got a divorce. Until I was ten, she dressed me like a boy – our neighbours thought I was a boy. It hid her shame and it protected me – but that also made me feel stronger inside. I can tap that strength to fight for Afghan women.

The day I turned fourteen, a palmist at the school fair predicted I'd get married before the year was out. Never, I told her. I'll make it to the highest office. I'm going to University. *(Beat)* That might happen too, she said calmly.

And it came to pass, just so. Mustafa saw me at my father's funeral and proposed. I agreed to marry him before I was 15, but only if he promised he'd let me get a degree. He kept his word, helped me realise my dreams. He's my sponsor, the father of my children, my mentor and my lover, all rolled into one. Raabia jan, he said, the Americans are kinder to Afghan women than their own. They've reserved half the seats in our parliament for women... success will come easier to you than me. And he was right. I'm on my way Madar-jaan. One final hurdle and I shall make it.

This woman at the hospital is right – child marriages are a key issue. What if I break the taboo and speak out against them? I'll work on Mustafa to get him to see it my way. "It's that final leap I need, Jaanum, to get women's votes Don't you see?"

SCENE FIFTEEN

Hospital patio. Saeed tries to phone Michael. Turns the music on. A few notes of Jenny's song from Scene One.

SCENE SIXTEEN

Saeed recalls a memory. Sound of flapping pigeons. Michael and Saeed are in Trafalgar Square, feeding them.

MICHAEL   Plenty of white pigeons in London. We'll find one like Afsar.

SAEED   Are there no shrines in London?

MICHAEL   Not those sort of shrines, Saeed. People come here to see Nelson's column.

Saeed throws some bird seed.

MICHAEL   He's so pesky, that baby grey. Isn't he?

SAEED   –

MICHAEL   He likes you, eh? He's fallen for that smile, Saeed...

SAEED   I like him too...

MICHAEL   Even though he's not white, like your Afsar? Hey? What's that?

SAEED   A bracelet. I wanted to put a ring on his leg...

MICHAEL   Can I see it? What is it?

Saeed stops wrestling with bracelet, gives it to him.

SAEED   A bunch of pigeon rings. For their feet.

MICHAEL   Goodness! Whoever heard of pigeon jewellery?

SAEED   Mum knows about it... and kaftar baazi...

Michael rattles the bracelet in his hand.

MICHAEL   Jenny wins hands down every time. Makes them noisy. No?

SAEED   We'd hear them at dawn, when they started tapping their feet on the rooftop, but they do go quiet in a raid.

MICHAEL   Here he is – back again

SAEED   He's like Cheekoo. Baba's grey messenger; he had a black and red stripe round his neck too.

MICHAEL   What was so special about Cheekoo? Did he ever tell you?

SAEED   When Baba was trapped behind the Russians, Cheekoo took a message across to his company and saved his life.

MICHAEL   So your Grandfather was a war hero?

SAEED   No. Cheekoo was. Baba always said I'd trust him with my life.

MICHAEL   They used carrier pigeons during both the World Wars, did you know?

Saeed drops the bracelet and chases the pigeon.

SCENE SEVENTEEN

Saeed's office at the MSF hospital. His beeper sounds. He speaks into it.

SAEED   Davies here (---) Right. I'll be there right away.

He picks up a stethoscope and dashes out. Raabia enters with a large box in her arms. She stands near his desk, hesitating. She carefully places the box on his table and looks around, fetches out her phone and reads messages.

Enter Saeed. He notices her and the box.

SAEED   Mrs. Durrani? What a pleasant surprise!

RAABIA   Mr. Davies asked me to organise this delivery for you...

SAEED   A huge box? For me? So sorry he put you to this trouble! May I open it?

RAABIA   Yes. It's definitely safe to open. It's been scanned twice.

SAEED   My birthday cake. Love the flags. Double chocolate, enriched with a double dose of radiation?

RAABIA   I assure you it's safest this way – when in Rome, as they say. Many happy returns of the day.

SAEED   Too old for birthdays but once you get used to them... I was sat outside missing the fuss Mum and Michael always made. Didn't know Michael had the cheek for a big ask like this.

RAABIA   To be fair, I offered. I persuaded him to let *The Times Magazine* interview him about my plan to bring Afghan professionals, creatives, thinkers and inspirers back home. They'll help us take that leap into the twenty-first century. We Afghan women need all the support we can get. Look! There's a card with it.

Raabia comes closer to him, reads the card.

RAABIA   Doctor S. K. Davies.

SAEED   A white pigeon bearing a message, catching up to Mum's level of detail, Michael? I'll call him soon to thank him. Many thanks again/

RAABIA   Please do. Tell him I kept my promise.

SAEED   I will.

RAABIA   My gift should have been your sister's address but we still can't trace her. Hoping we'll get lucky soon.

SAEED   With my luck?

RAABIA   Nothing wrong with your luck! You were born a man, you made it to London. I'd say wait, before you begin to despair.

Saeed looks at her blankly.

SAEED   I've been here too long... I miss the rain, I'm tired of the sunshine and endless casualties and I still can't imagine meeting her ...

RAABIA   It might happen, one day when you least expect it. Please come to dine with us on Friday. Mustafa's inviting you to/

SAEED   Thank you. That's very kind of him.

RAABIA   No, that's not good enough, Saeed. You have to accept. Attend my public meeting. Bring anyone you want to. Maybe, the counsellor, whose campaign you mentioned, will come?

SAEED   She might not be willing to go to crowded public events.

RAABIA   Please do ask her. We never get enough females out... It's more than politics, women's lives are at stake.

RAABIA   As for her campaign, do tell her I admire her insight and courage. But when I consulted Mustafa about child marriages, he said. 'Best to go carefully with that one. Women's issues are controversial, definite vote-losers. And feelings run high when religious beliefs are threatened.'

SAEED   It's more cultural than religious.

RAABIA   And I said to him, 'Husband, no pain, no gain!' I'm ready to start on this one, Saeed, even if he isn't. More women are voting now anyway… so it's fine. No?

SAEED   Only if they're free to choose who they vote for…Would be great to see you raise the issue. I'll help, if I can, of course.

RAABIA   I'm launching my campaign at a huge rally after Friday prayers. Big step-change for my profile. I'll focus on women's rights. We'll send out leaflets. Here's a VIP invitation for you and the counsellor.

SAEED   Anything for a good cause! Thanks for all your trouble with the cake…

RAABIA   Pleasure. Wish I had the time to watch you cut it. I wondered which flag you'd pick…

SAEED (*flustered*) You did? Hmm… both, of course.

RAABIA   Nearly got you there! I have to attend a meeting at the Party HQ. Got to rush. I'm so sorry.

SAEED   So am I! Good luck with it all, Mrs. Durrani.

Exit Raabia. Saeed picks up a pigeon bracelet on his desk, gazes at it. Pigeons coo faintly. Nazneen enters, notices the bracelet.

NAZNEEN   Is that yours, Doctor? I had/

Saeed pockets it, embarrassed.

SAEED   An old keepsake…

NAZNEEN   That was Mrs. Durrani, right?

SAEED   Yes. She brought this chocolate cake for me, and a VIP invitation for you and me.

NAZNEEN   That's great. So she'll talk about child marriages in a big way, will she?

SAEED   Umm... *(reads the invite)*

NAZNEEN   And no mention of a major issue? What did I tell you?

SAEED   She'll move slowly, even stealthily, if she can.

NAZNEEN   I expected more from her. Her father switched parties, you know/

SAEED   I wouldn't get historical, Mrs. Ekram, the past is a jungle full of demons...

NAZNEEN   Jungles are full of animals, and butterflies, and gentle birds, like doves and pigeons, Doctor Davies, not demons/

SAEED   True. Demons live among people or inside their heads – that's what my grandfather used to say.

NAZNEEN   So did mine/

SAEED   Reckon all grandfathers must say things like that!

NAZNEEN   Of course – the guardians of tradition, aren't they?

SAEED   Do you think you'll come?

NAZNEEN   I should, shouldn't I?

SAEED   To ask difficult questions, you mean?

NAZNEEN   Yes. Maybe. I am tempted to –.

SAEED   She needs supporters, not hecklers, but she did ask for you.

NAZNEEN   I'll think about it.

SAEED   Let me know. Maybe we could go together? Would you take this cake home, Mrs. Ekram? Might get wasted here.

NAZNEEN   Are you sure? My children would love it/

SAEED   How old are they?

NAZNEEN   My son's five, and my daughter is nine. Here they are...

She flips open her bag and holds out a photo.

SAEED   Beautiful kids!

NAZNEEN   Thank you. I think so too, Mashallah.. Mona and Zafar.

SAEED   Zafar? I had a.../

A happy trill of flute playing.

NAZNEEN   I must go and see Mansoor. He's being released tomorrow.

SAEED   Great news.

NAZNEEN   He sounds happy but I... I am not sure it's right.

SAEED   It's a happier sound – what's your worry?

NAZNEEN   I'm not sure he's ready...

SAEED   He'll cope. He was never cossetted much, was he?

NAZNEEN   That's true. One too many for his own family. *(Beat)* Thank you for the cake.

Nazneen tries to fit the cake in a tote bag. She brings out her knitting, forgets it on the table.

Exit Nazneen.

Saeed turns, spots the knitting and picks it up.

SAEED   Mrs. Ekram! Don't forget your... *(Pause)* I learnt to knit – nearly ...

SCENE EIGHTEEN

At the rally. Change of lights and music. A lively song by Ariana Sayeed is playing. Raabia, Saeed and Nazneen are waiting to speak.

RAABIA   Welcome, welcome! Glad you came too...?

SAEED   Mrs. Ekram, my colleague, the counsellor who/

RAABIA   Mrs. Ekram. Of course. Forgive me, I guessed, but the name kept slipping out of my reach.

NAZNEEN   You meet hundreds of people. I'll come and hound you again and again, so you learn my name.

RAABIA   I agree with you, Mrs. Ekram, in principle. I really do.

NAZNEEN   We both tried to get others to come ... but they're all nervous of local crowds ... mostly they're foreigners on the team... you know what they're like...

SAEED   Ahem.

NAZNEEN   Sorry. That came out wrong... I had to come because I feel so strongly about child marriages. That's why I asked Dr. Davies to plead my case/

RAABIA   It's the biggest issue holding our women back. Absolutely. But if you're in politics, you know it's a long game, like chess/

SAEED   Guess your plan is to build the strength of the movement first, if I may speak for you?

RAABIA   Exactly. And we do need ambassadors like you two, to raise consciousness about these issues. So thank you.

NAZNEEN   I'll volunteer for you, if you do raise it, loudly enough. *(Beat)* Thank you for all you do, but this is the tradition that warped my life. It affected me personally. I don't want my daughter or her generation to suffer/

RAABIA   I understand your passion. I think we should use it and your rage to good effect. Would you agree, Saeed?

NAZNEEN   The men will resist, I fear...

SAEED   Not all men.

RAABIA   To be honest, Mustafa did – but I think he genuinely fears for our safety... In the centre of Kabul, inside this ring of steel, we're safe. Beyond that, he says, extremists won't let anyone challenge their dominance over women. Campaigning for women's rights draws out the real fanatics. They turn reform into a theological issue and call it blasphemy.

NAZNEEN   Some causes are worth dying for.

SAEED   That's what the fanatics say. We're on the side of life, Mrs. Ekram. Being safe is something you owe yourself/

NAZNEEN   Sure. Me and my children. I don't want to die – but we can't live in terrror. I want the same rights for Mona as my son.

RAABIA   I understand. You're a survivor... your testimony is worth a thousand words. We should let you speak about this, Mrs. Ekram.

NAZNEEN   You'd say it so much better than me...

RAABIA   I'm an enabler. You can do it. Just tell your story in your own words. People will be moved to hear it from your lips. *(Raabia steps up to the mic')*

Friends, honoured guests, allow me to introduce Mrs. Ekram, a dear friend, a counsellor and a passionate campaigner. She's going to share her story with us today to raise awareness of an issue that's huge for Afghan women: early marriages.

Nazneen steps up to the mic' and addresses the crowd.

NAZNEEN   I learnt as a little girl that boys are more special than girls. But the day my older brother died, though she tried to hide it, my mother's eyes asked a question that broke my heart: 'Why couldn't it be you?' they said. My younger brother rose two pegs higher that day. She and my grandfather took to spoiling him and turned him into a little tyrant.

Our father had already passed... our lands were lost during the invasion. With no wages coming in, money got tighter. I was the one who always went without new books, new clothes, new shoes, but when Moray pulled me out of school, days before the final exams, I was more angry than sad. My little brother, bless him, tried hard to comfort me that day... with his collection of marbles, with pigeon bells and packets of sugared almonds. Nothing consoled me.

Then came the day when Baba said that asylum in Europe was the only way of saving my brother's life, and Moray simply nodded her agreement. Baba thought he could sell his house and land to pay for it, but dying farms fetch nothing during a siege. So, he came up with another idea.

When Moray asked me how I felt about getting married, I had very little to fight back with... 'I can knit and sew,' I said, 'to pay for my keep'.

And Moray said. 'I know. But the bride price Ekram's offered for you can buy your brother a place on the truck leaving for Europe this month. It's the only way to save him.

This Ekram seems a good man. He will look after you, always, I'm sure. Maybe they would even let us stall and delay the wedding for a year?'

I couldn't defend myself then. Nor could she, had she wanted to, nor my little brother... Saadi...

Saeed looks up at her, recognises her.

Pistol shots. Sirens and whistles.

Blackout.

SCENE NINETEEN

Lights up to reveal Saeed packing. Enter Nazneen. She waves a knitted scarf at him.

NAZNEEN   It's done. I never thought I'd finish in time...

SAEED   Exactly like the one I lost on the trek. Where did you get this pattern?

NAZNEEN Remember the old killim rug in our neighbour's house? *(Pause)*

SAEED No... but I saw one recently and wondered why it looked so familiar. I'm amazed you remembered how to make it.

NAZNEEN Your fingers remember the moves. Don't lose it again, though.

SAEED I won't, I promise you. *(Beat)* Amazing how easily you've flipped from polite colleague to bossy big sister. *(Beat)* Maybe sibling rivalry has muscle memory too?

NAZNEEN Why else would you shatter every single memory I've held on to for years?

NAZNEEN Wasn't easy... She got me to speak out. I'd no idea I was going to. I didn't know you were there, Saeed... I might not have said it all...

SAEED And I'd never have known the truth about the past... If only ... I could make up for it, somehow/

NAZNEEN Look ahead, Saadi. *We* found each other.

SAEED Yes – and we must hold on to each other. To make sure what happened to you mustn't happen to Mona.

NAZNEEN I'll fight for her to my last breath.

SAEED Be careful, Naz – they need you – both of them/

NAZNEEN I know... I wish you weren't rushing back so soon.

SAEED Does feel a bit too soon, now. But I panicked. Couldn't take it all – my country, my homeland, my people, full on, in the raw.

NAZNEEN   It's not easy, surviving out here.

SAEED   There are positive reasons pulling me back too. I miss my job, my friends, my home and Michael, most of all. Never thought I would. *(Pause)* I wish you'd agreed to talk to the immigration lawyers he found for you... We'll both worry about you.

NAZNEEN   I'll miss you, Saeed. But I must protect my children from any more risks and disruptions.

SAEED   Have those threatening phone calls stopped?

NAZNEEN   I changed my phone number. *(Beat)* Sent you a text from the new one. I'm thinking... of moving - maybe even changing my name...

SAEED   Awful! To be forced to hide for daring to speak the truth. That's what I hate the most out here now... Poor Mrs. Durrani paid the ultimate price – killed for trying to change things...

NAZNEEN   Every day I tell myself it's not my fault but when I'm alone, I see her eyes glazed in shock, blood gushing from her throat...

SAEED   I'm the same. Every morning, every single night, I see her.

NAZNEEN   Keep your eye on the future. That's the advice from the party –

SAEED   You joined her party?

NAZNEEN   The least I could do. *(Beat)*

SAEED   Sometimes you can be more effective outside the system. *(Beat)* And you know Michael said you do qualify for asylum.

NAZNEEN   I couldn't leave here, Saeed. But don't forget about us.

SAEED   I just couldn't bear another loss, another tragedy. But I'm not doing a runner. I'll work on building that medical liaison link.

NAZNEEN   We will change things for women here, even if it goes slowly. Maybe Mrs. Durrani can see us from wherever she is/

SAEED   Never thought it could end like this! She seemed so powerful, so successful. What's life trying to teach me, Naz?

NAZNEEN   That there are no guarantees. And, that sometimes, strangers do more for us than our own flesh and blood.

SAEED   I learnt that one early, with Michael and Jenny. Without them, I'd have lost it after that terrible journey. Michael offered to come over, to be here with me, even though he hates flying. But I told him I do have some family here now –

NAZNEEN   Look what I found today.

She holds up her pigeon anklets. He looks at them, takes his bracelet out of his pocket.

SAEED   Almost identical – but not quite. Keep mine, so you can give one to Mona and one to Zafar. *(Pulls out an envelope with money)* And this.

Nazneen is reluctant to take it.

NAZNEEN   We're fine now, Saeed...

SAEED   ... it's for them... with so much love, from an uncle, lost across the black waters –

It's only what I can do now but I promise I'll always be there for them. You can count on me.

Nazneen moves forward to hug him.

SCENE TWENTY

SAEED When I rang Michael to say, 'I'm coming home,' the relief and joy in his voice cheered me no end.

My hardest day in Kabul was long and painful; Nazneen and I attended Mrs. Durrani's funeral. Naz said some healing and brave words to her shocked husband. I felt proud of her wisdom, her courage. Now, I'll miss her more than I did, when I could hardly remember her. I'll miss her as the friend I got to know, before I knew her...

Michael couldn't understand why Naz won't send her children far away from danger to a land where they can live in peace. 'Mad to be so committed to the soil,' he said. Yes, and she's crazy to be an optimist in these dark times, I know, but I do respect her wishes. I stand by her. She has faith in her God but also in her cause, and in herself and in the future.

Lights down.

The end.

Above: Jay Varsani and John O'Mahony   Photo: Robert Day

Above: Jay Varsani and Suzanne Ahmet   Photo: Robert Day

Aurora Metro Books

HAMLET adapted by Mark Norfolk
ISBN 978-1-911501-01-5   £9.99

COMBUSTION by Asif Khan
ISBN 978-1-911501-91-6   £9.99

DIARY OF A HOUNSLOW GIRL by Ambreen Razia
ISBN 978-0-9536757-9-1   £8.99

SPLIT/MIXED by Ery Nzaramba
ISBN 978-1-911501-97-8   £10.99

THE TROUBLE WITH ASIAN MEN by Sudha Bhuchar, Kristine
Landon-Smith and Louise Wallinger
ISBN 978-1-906582-41-8   £8.99

SOUTHEAST ASIAN PLAYS ed. Cheryl Robson and Aubrey Mellor
ISBN 978-1-906582-86-9   £16.99

SIX PLAYS BY BLACK AND ASIAN WOMEN WRITERS ed. Kadija
George
ISBN 978-0-9515877-2-0   £12.99

DURBAN DIALOGUES, INDIAN VOICE by Ashwin Singh
ISBN 978-1-906582-42-5   £15.99

WOMEN OF ASIA by Asa Palomera
ISBN 978-1-906582-94-4   £7.99

HARVEST by Manjula Padmanabhan
ISBN 978-0-9536757-7-7   £6.99

I HAVE BEFORE ME A REMARKABLE DOCUMENT by Sonja Linden
ISBN 978-0-9546912-3-3   £7.99

THE IRANIAN FEAST by Kevin Dyer
ISBN 978-1-910798-93-5   £8.99

NEW SOUTH AFRICAN PLAYS ed. Charles J. Fourie
ISBN 978-0-9542330-1-3   £11.99

BLACK AND ASIAN PLAYS Anthology introduced by Afia Nkrumah
ISBN 978-0-9536757-4-6   £12.99

www.aurorametro.com